SANCTUARY

Illustrations by AMBER DAY

SANCTUARY

> ———————————————————— <

Inside the pages of this book you'll find rooms filled with elaborate textiles, cozy kitchens, a few patterns, creative work spaces, dream closets, bohemian patios, and secret hideaways.

You'll notice that several pages of this book have empty spaces left for you to fill if you are feeling creative. Explore your inner artist and try drawing the chair you're sitting on right now, your favorite embroidered pillow from the flea market, that rug you saw on vacation in Morocco, or your furry best friend.

Published in 2016 by Designxiety Press

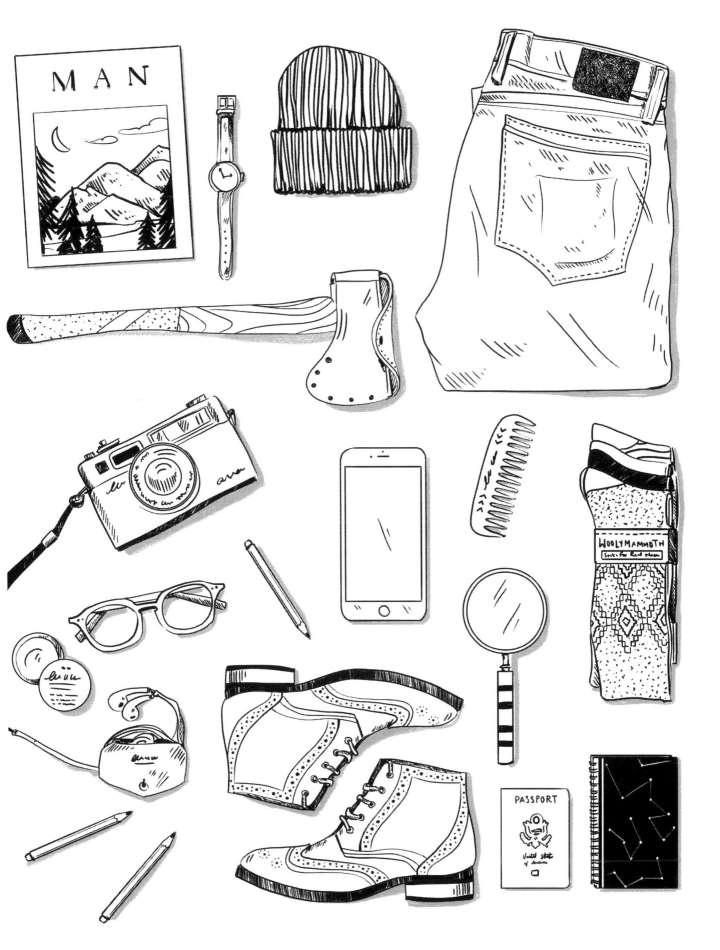

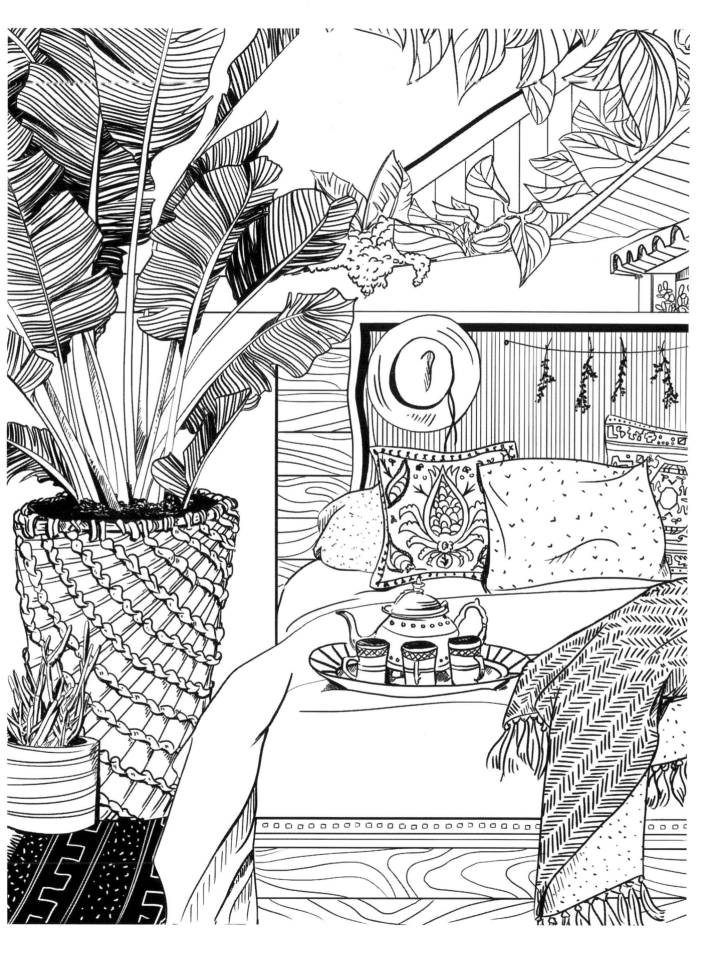

CREATE YOUR OWN SANCTUARY

CREATE YOUR OWN SANCTUARY

Illustrator Amber Day grew up in Tempe, Arizona, surrounded by Southwestern textiles, desert inspired interiors, and beautiful mountain landscapes. Upon graduating high school, she attended a design college in downtown LA , studying visual design and communications. Combining her love of interiors, a background in fashion and textiles, and illustration, she created SANCTUARY.

Visit Amber online at designxiety.com

Made in the USA
Las Vegas, NV
13 December 2021

37427134R00031